How to

Act

IN BUSINESS

Corey Hansen

ISBN: 978-0-9841541-0-4

"How to Act in Business" and the author are available for special
promotions, premiums, customized training and speaking events.
For details contact Corey Hansen at www.howtoactinbusiness.com

Third Edition

*With deep gratitude to my teachers and muses,
especially Mom, Dad, Maren, Will, Kim, and Jean*

Preface

Leaving a life in the theatre I realized I was entering new territory, the corporate stage. What would I have to offer? Would I succeed? I knew it was the right thing to do for my personal situation but found myself nervously approaching this new life.

After a few weeks the actor in me started to notice the way people in the business world interacted with each other. As I observed this, the thought kept coming to me: *If they only knew some of the techniques we use in the theatre they'd be so much more effective at what they do.*

Presented here is a retelling of what occurred in an actual coaching session. The concept of using theatre-based techniques naturally emerged from the conversation and I found that the dialogue I'd been having in my head was now coming out. And it proved effective.

In that session I realized there is a fundamental element to communication with others--the action--that I'd been studying and practicing in the studio and on stage for years. If that element is appropriate for the situation we're in we should be in good shape as we pursue key relationships and goals.

I chose to write "How to Act in Business" in play-script format to best represent the dialogue presented in the coaching session that day. This may be new for readers so some guidelines seem appropriate here:

Phrases in *(parentheses and italics)* represent stage directions so we get a sense of where the character is in space and what they may be experiencing, e.g. *(silence)*. Also, they can represent the attitude or action with which the character is speaking. This is designed to give the reader (actor!) clues as to how to play the part but in no way are dictating how the performance should go. That is up to you as the actor and, of course, it is your interpretation that is most important!

Subject Headings, e.g. (ACTIONS DEFINED) in all caps are normally not part of a script. I added them as a guide for easier recall and access to ideas that are important to you.

Character names are at the beginning of each line, in this case only two characters: Bob and Coach.

Graphics are inserted for clarity of ideas and as tools for you and are normally not part of a script.

At the end of the book is a list of actions for your creative thought process. It is not an exhaustive list of all the verbs available to us to play but rather representative. As you'll learn in the dialogue, role can emerge from action and action can inform role. I thought you might like to sample some actions that could work for you in your world.

The basis of this guide to better interaction is the "4-A Way of Communicating" an easy to understand and use model of structuring or reviewing communication. I created the "4-A Way" based on observation of the best and most challenged communicators:

AUDIENCE	ATMOSPHERE
What do I want from my audience? They from me?	What is the overall energy surrounding this interaction?

ACTOR	ACTION
Does my energy in body, voice, and intention support the action?	What am I doing to my audience to help us get what we want?

I trust you'll find the model helpful as you continue on the path of building your skills as a communicator.

Thank you for the opportunity to share "How to Act in Business" with you.

Contents

<u>Cast</u>

Bob
Coach

(Walking into Bob's office we see a u-shaped desk, high-back leather desk chair, two guest chairs. On his desk are standard leader-type things: laptop, phone, desk accessories, some piles, ink blotter/calendar, notebooks with pens, water bottle, and a bitten styrofoam coffee cup. On the walls a whiteboard, a few pictures and a window. Marketing items from past promotions dominate the corner with adorning flower clock, a real flowering plant, and in another corner a bookshelf with more piles. A new, somewhat intense leader, Bob, talks with his Coach about strategies to get to the next level. We join them mid-conversation.)

ACTIONS DEFINED

BOB: What I need to do is think about not just the next level, but the level above that.

(Bob draws a chart on his whiteboard with boxes representing each group of executives, junior, mid-level, and senior.)

BOB: *(circling the "senior" box)* Those are the guys I need to worry about.

COACH: *(nudging Bob into discussion)* I think it's interesting the word choices people use. It may seem picky to you, but I noticed you said the word "worry", as in, "those are the guys I need to worry about". Action words are very important in what we do and how we act. You recall from when we met awhile back that I have a background in the professional theatre?

BOB: *(pressing)* Yes. And we both have cats and like cheese. So?

COACH: As actors on the stage, we play actions. That's what we do to get done what we need to get done in a play. We carefully choose the actions we are going to play. In this case, what might be other action words, verbs, you could use instead of "worry"?

(A suspicious "are we wasting time here" stare from Bob)

COACH: *(patiently)* I mean, what do you do to that audience to engage with them? Do you worry?

(Pause. Nothing from Bob)

COACH: Do you challenge them? Enthuse? Energize?

(Bob turns away from his whiteboard and pursuing coach and slowly makes his way into his chair not knowing what to say)

COACH: The best actors play actions to get what they want and the very best change their actions frequently. I've always admired Sally Field in the graveyard scene from "Steel Magnolias". She has a monologue where she changes actions a dozen times very quickly. Absolutely compelling. The actor's process is to structure action that is appropriate to where they are and what they're doing in a play. They also want to make it interesting and unpredictable for their audience. The more they change the more interesting it is. In order to change quickly though, you have to have a list of actions from which to choose.

BOB: *(still suspecting, hesitantly)* So, rather than worry… I can choose what action to use in moving to the next level?

COACH: *(matter of fact)* Yes. And it always depends on what you're trying to accomplish in your business, or on the stage.

(The Coach gets up, takes a marker and moves to Bob's cluttered whiteboard, borrowing a bit of space)

STRUCTURE OF ACTION

COACH: The best actors rarely use a formal

system to determine action in a scene--they do it intuitively. That's their talent. But sometimes scenes are so complex that a system helps them structure the action.

(Drawing a chart on the whiteboard with three columns. Bob is bristling a bit, and yet, is intrigued.)

COACH: Here's a simple structure I've used in playing complex roles. Over on the right side of my script is the text, like the dialogue we're having now--the character's lines, where I move, and other staging notes. But on the left side of my script is where the real work comes in, this structure of action I've been talking about *(starting to fill in the chart)*. The column closest to the text is what I call my "overall want". It's what my character wants in life. The middle column is the "immediate want". Here I list what my character wants in the particular scene I'm in. This can change every so often depending on where the scene goes.

Action	Immediate Want	Overall Want

BOB: *(a brightening interest)* And that adds to the audience's engagement.

COACH: Yes, and the left "action" column changes even more frequently. This is where I list the actions, the verbs that I am going to play. Changing them most frequently allows for very dynamic interaction that keeps an audience interested, and guessing.

(Bob is looking more engaged and starts to smile with a slight look of amazement on his face)

BOB: *(suddenly grabbing his notebook and fumbling for a pen)* This is incredible!

COACH: *(surprised by Bob's sudden burst of energy)* Incredible? There's a lot more here to…

BOB: *(writing feverishly)* They don't teach you this stuff in B-school!

COACH: *(leveraging Bob's energy)* And, this works well because it is totally intuitive *(crossing back to his chair, sitting, relaxed and easy)*. It's our talent as human beings. We play actions all the time and respond to actions all the time. It's what we do to interact. And we're successful at it most of the time.

BOB: *(leaning in past his water bottle, pen paused)* So "worry" may not work for what I'm trying to do.

COACH: *(leaning in to match Bob's growing interest)* "Worry" may be the right action for you and the "play" you're in, but that action seems to be more inward directed than out toward the audience you're playing with. The thing about playing actions is, the action is always directed toward someone. You are doing something to someone else when you play actions. Even when Shakespeare's Hamlet is alone on stage in a soliloquy, he has audience in mind. His mother, father, uncle, Ophelia, Horatio--all these can come flying into his mind at any time and his action, even while alone, can be directed to them. Whether consciously or subconsciously, we direct our action to the appropriate recipient even if they're not there with us.

DETERMINING ACTIONS

BOB: *(risking it)* Let me try this on. In thinking about the presentations and meetings I do, I guess I mostly inform, educate...

COACH: *(with a wry smile)* That's boring.

BOB: ...and try to impress.

COACH: 'Impress' is an interesting action. Last year I got a call from a consultant who said she had a case for me that she was having trouble solving. She said that a client started to feel like he couldn't breathe during a major presentation. I called the man and sure enough, he said it felt like his throat was closing off. He had to excuse himself from the meeting and splash cold water on his face to get to where he could come back to the meeting table!

BOB: I can sympathize. What caused it?

COACH: The man, an account manager for his company, was involved in a meeting with his senior executive team and their contemporaries from a major client, a huge opportunity. The account manager's role was to introduce each group to the other and take action items. When he went to speak, he had difficulty and then had to leave the room to get his breath back. But it wasn't until he told me that "I just wanted to impress everybody there" that I realized he got caught up in playing the wrong action. Listen to what he said: *"My job was to make introductions and take action items."* And somewhere along the line he added another significant task--to impress! This action, directed toward the meeting attendees, caused way too much stress, and, most critically was the *wrong action*. It wasn't even close to playing the two assigned actions of "to introduce" and "to take action items". And how was he supposed to know if he was successful in his attempt to impress?

BOB: *(adjusting back in his chair)* So, impressing is wrong? Isn't that what you have to do if you want to move up?

COACH: It's important to make positive impressions, and there's nothing wrong with someone saying they are impressed with you. But how do you make a good impression with people?

BOB: You do good work I suppose.

COACH: Yes, and what part of doing good work includes impressing someone, I mean if you're really focused on doing good work?

(pause—Bob considers, back and forth between buying this or not, his initial excitement waning)

BOB: *(a bit self-conscious)* None of it, I guess.

COACH: But focusing on the actions one plays that end up being impressive is a productive way to go because you can do something about that.

HOW TO PLAY ACTIONS

BOB: I'm not so sure I understand how I play actions, though.

COACH: The true test of a great action is whether or not you can do it right now. If I said to you, play "to challenge" could you do it to me right now?

BOB: *(dryly, lifting the bitten cup to his mouth)* Yeah, I'd probably ask you why in the world you wore that shirt.

COACH: *(enjoying the wit)* Now in playing that action you might be described as a challenging person or difficult or maybe a jokester. These are qualities that can describe others, but they are very difficult to play. It's like a stage director coming and telling me that I need to be very "impressive" in this scene. That's great, and I may have a sense of what that looks and feels like. But more often than not, especially with less experienced or talented actors, their version of impressive will come off as a caricature--it's a sketch of what someone who's impressive *is* and we don't believe it as an audience. The best actors immediately realize, whether by instinct or through their craft, that they've got to figure out what a person who impresses does to other people. Do they instruct, alert, challenge, honor, confront, encourage, or build up? *(Bob considers)* So when a director comes to me and says "be happy" in this scene, I work a system where I think of all the things that someone who is happy *does* to other people--in other words, what actions they play.

BOB: *(getting the gist of it)* So maybe, in my view of what I do with senior leaders, I tend to go after something that is fairly boring, like, "inform" or "educate" when what I really need to do is something more radical, I mean… just go for it.

COACH: You'll have to tell me what "go for it" means to you.

BOB: I would guess it's a lot like the difference between being behind the scenes and on the stage. There's a point where you have to go on stage and then you've got to *(a fisted gesture for emphasis)* go for it! I mean, what's the worse thing that can happen out there--you die?

COACH: *(teasing)* If you died you wouldn't care. Throwing up is probably the worst thing you can do.

BOB: *(enjoying this)* All right, so if in my scenario of getting to the top level what's the worst thing that can happen to me? I drool, lose my thoughts, which happens to me when I'm tired, or make a fool of myself. I suppose those would be the worst things so why not just go for it? *(standing with a big gesture and slightly maniacal smile, with a louder voice, risking being heard by those outside his closed-door office)* I don't just want to be average, I want to be a leader! I want to lead people places where they didn't think they could go!

COACH: *(matching Bob's energy, on his feet now as well)* So go ahead, lead!

BOB: *(smile held but not energized)* Right now?

COACH: *(not letting up)* Yes. Can you do it right now?

BOB: *(pause, quiet, kid-like)* I don't really know how to lead *right now*.

COACH: Well, you could lead a dog around your office here couldn't you?

BOB: Yes, but that's not the kind of leading I mean of course.

COACH: Of course *(slowly sitting on the edge of his chair, quietly intense).* So think about what we said earlier: You should be able to play the action you choose immediately. It should be natural. It should come out in your voice and body!

BOB: I don't know what to do *(a slight attempt at gaining sympathy).* Actions are kind of tough for me.

COACH: And challenging for me as I learned the actor's process. Still is today. It's tough to define what we do naturally. It's like asking a great athlete or singer "how do you do that?" Often they won't know—they just do it.

BOB: Like one of my team who is awesome at financial modeling. I couldn't touch that stuff and they make it look easy! Seems like it's what they're meant to do.

COACH: And I always envied the really great actors who just naturally respond to a situation. They say their lines as if they always said them that way. Though they do need some process to get through the tough spots in the script sometimes.

BOB: So they look to these actions?

COACH: Yes. *(encouraging)* Now you're getting a feel for what an actor goes through *(standing, playing the "Director")*. The director says "be a leader" in this scene and you sort of take a stab at stuff that a leader does--maybe puff your chest out a bit, use a commanding voice, smoke cigars, mostly external stuff--and the director goes back to their seat and watches to see if you got what they're looking for. So now, Bob, *(progressively louder and in Bob's face)* you're the actor and you've got to come up with a believable Leader and the pressure is on with only one week left of rehearsal and you're STILL not GETTING THIS SCENE and EVERYONE IS WATCHING YOU and you KNOW you're WASTING THEIR TIME, so will you JUST ACT LIKE A LEADER!

(long pause)

BUILDING A REPERTOIRE OF ACTIONS

BOB: *(quietly)* A leader challenges.

COACH: Yes?

BOB: A leader gets people to see their vision.

COACH: What else?

BOB: *(gaining momentum)* A leader confronts, and inspires.

COACH: I'd want to know more about "inspires" 'cause it's big but go ahead.

BOB: In the stuff I deliver, like this presentation here, *(sliding over a pile of paper)* I really do a lot of informing.

COACH: *(challenging, to leverage the momentum)* Is there more that you do beyond "inform"? What are you DOING to those senior executives that you want to be? Enthusing? Exciting?

BOB: *(cautiously)* I energize.

COACH: Great *(writing in his book).* What else?

BOB: I titillate.

COACH: You titillate?

BOB: Titillate.

(pause)

COACH: *(holding back a smile)* You titillate.

BOB: I titillate.

(pause)

COACH: *(slowly)* You're telling me, that you, an executive inside of a major international company with billions in revenues are actually coming to work and titillating?!

BOB: Yeah, we put a slide in the presentation to titillate them. I knew that would titillate them.

COACH: You're smiling at that.

BOB: Yes, it's fun and it was there to make a point and let them laugh a bit which we really need right now.

COACH: *(enjoying the imagination)* So you encourage, enthuse, and...titillate.

BOB: Yes, I guess I do. I never thought about it like that. *(big, unexpected smile, his energy back)* This is great *(quickly jotting something in his notebook)*!

COACH: *(building on the enthusiasm, trying not to interrupt Bob's writing)* You're starting to build a repertoire of actions. Like any great performer, athlete, or a parent, you have a list of things whether conscious or not that you can *do* at any moment depending on the audience. The great ones have them available at all times and know how to play them. Some are risky and many are safe. In business we tend to play the safe ones so we don't offend, and yet people are people and they really are much more engaged if you play a variety of actions.

BOB: But I don't want to come off as phony! If I play all these actions I might not be very good at some and then feel uncomfortable.

COMFORT ZONES AND BELIEVABILITY

COACH: The discomfort is a natural part of learning something new and it's a good thing, Bob. It's the gap you feel in your head, heart, or gut between what you know how to do and what you don't--you're stretching to fill the gap and that's uncomfortable. You never want to come off as phony though.

BOB: Of course not *(swirling his coffee to get the last bit of flavor).* You could ruin your credibility in one conversation.

COACH: Believability is the bottom line. Certainly in the theatre. I've been not believable at home a few times and definitely got called on that.

BOB: Definitely!

COACH: And at work it's the same thing. So, like the actor who is focused on the immediate or overall objectives of the character, your action is always focused on the business objectives of your customers, the company, your organization, your group, and individuals--like the person with whom you're playing actions *(Bob jots down a thought in his notebook)*. If they look across at you and don't believe you, it's over. So yes--you have to take a risk sometimes in playing actions that are outside your comfort zone. Believability is rooted in the sincerity with which you play your actions. Too much or too little energy and the recipient of your action, your audience, will not buy it.

BOB: It takes some practice doesn't it.

COACH: *(smiling)* Isn't that what we're constantly doing, practicing this stuff with people and finding the best way to work with them?

BOB: *(excited)* Yeah, but I've never thought of it in these terms before. They do not teach this to you in B-school, that's for sure! I think all in all that everybody is just acting anyway--playing different roles, dressing the part, acting like everything's okay when it's not. It's quite a performance.

DETERMINING ROLE – BREAKING PERFORMANCE INTO MANAGEABLE PARTS

COACH: By understanding the actions you play you can figure out your role. If you "challenge" you become a "Challenger". If you "coerce" you're the great "Coerce-er". And if you want your people to be "inspired"--remember, that's a quality or state of being and tough to play--you best be busy as an "Inspirer" yourself. So role quickly follows action, or vice versa.

BOB: *(checking his notes)* This isn't easy. I can see how there's some art to this, and I see the science in it too.

COACH: I think I tend to experience the art of it. Tell me more about the science.

BOB: All things have a science to them. Think about the pianist who sets about to play a concerto. They've got the music, a structure, a science to it. You can take it apart and see the separate notes, even the way that when I press a key on the piano *(Bob presses an imaginary piano key on his desk)* the hammer strikes a string and makes a vibration that travels through the air--that's all science stuff. And in order to really play the thing they've got to get down to manageable parts.

COACH: So you play?

BOB: Used to. My daughter's really into it now.

COACH: Ahh.

BOB: My daughter tells me that musicians who are having difficulty with a part of the music slow it way down and study, pretty much, the science of it, one slow step at a time.

COACH: Very interesting. It's the same way with the actor who is having a tough time with a complex part. They break down what's happening and study each part--the words, scene structure, intent of the playwright, and as we talked about earlier, they apply a system of action to help them through. In short, they study the action of it. Is that what you're talking about when you say the science of this?

BOB: Yes, exactly. But then at some point, the pianist or actor or athlete has to play the piece, play the play, play the game *(now playing his desk like a keyboard with both hands)*. They can't stay stuck in the science of it or people will probably see their technique instead of hearing the music! Nobody wants to see how you do it. I mean they may wonder at some point how the person did it. It's like watching a great magician, marveling at the illusion, and then marveling again afterward about how they could have possibly done what they did. So there's a mix back and forth between art and science. *(pause)* An artfulness to being a leader and an actor. The leader as an actor *(making a note in his book)*.

COACH: *(impressed, taking it in, making a note in his book)* Perhaps so.

BOB: I haven't thought of it like that before. Could you be an actor/leader?

COACH: *(laughing)* I see it all the time! I'm just not sure anyone knows they're doing it.

BOB: So you see more science than art?

COACH: Maybe so! I know that the technique is there for you when the art isn't happening.

BOB: So I can fall back on that when interacting with people.

COACH: Sure. You can even practice playing actions while you're getting your work done.

PRACTICING PLAYING ACTIONS

BOB: How's that work?

COACH: You choose something you're going to work on the next time you have an interaction. Say that it's more difficult for you to confront someone. The action is "confront" but it's never been easy for you, and approaching the interaction is causing some anxiety--a natural response when we go to do something we're unsure of. So, you consciously decide to prepare and practice being a "Confronter". You break that down into the science of confrontation, get the steps down and structure your sense of how the action needs to go.

Then you practice it with someone or alone. When you go to do the real interaction you give yourself a break, understand your potential anxiety, and continue practicing the technique during the interaction until it starts to flow as a more artful interaction. Over time confronting isn't such a big deal any more and you start to enjoy the art of it.

BOB: *(cynically)* Like there is ever going to be enjoyment in confronting someone.

COACH: The outcome may lend itself to joy, yes? A way to look at this *(he approaches the whiteboard)* is to list the roles, based on actions, that you feel comfortable playing and those you don't. Just start with a list based on what you know about yourself and feedback from others. You're seeking feedback from others?

BOB: Yes...well, sometimes.

COACH: That's something critical to knowing if the actions you're playing are working. Ask for feedback, and even tell the person what you're working on so they can specifically watch for it over time.

BOB: Needs to be someone I trust.

COACH: You bet. And it should be someone who has a stake is your success, whether a manager, peer, or someone who reports to you. As you approach this

you'll want to think about what roles you're
comfortable with and those you'd like to grow into
(*drawing a chart on the whiteboard*). So in this
example there's one role you feel comfortable with and
one you need to work on:

Comfortable	Uncomfortable	Transitional actions
Encourager	Challenger	Invite Encourage Honor Listen (activity) Build up Challenge

COACH: *(continued)* Transitional actions allow you to
approach the uncomfortable action/role in steps. You
probably don't want to come out challenging someone
from the start. You might first invite the person to the
conversation, encourage them to be honest, honor them
by making good eye contact, and use an assuring smile
while listening closely. One of the actions you might
use is what you do well—you "encourage". What
you're creating here is a kind of barometer measuring
where you are today and where you want to go. It's
great for planning your development. And your trusted
colleagues, friend, or family can be a meter for how
you're progressing.

BOB: And if I don't know how to do something? To play a certain action or act the way I want?

COACH: Think about those you work with who are good at the role you're pursuing. What do they do, specifically, in voice and body? Mimic them. Another idea is to work with me or someone you trust to practice playing this sequence of actions. The point here is, you've got to practice. I think you'll find you do this naturally, but practicing is what lets you know if it feels right or not and lets the words you say start to match up with your actions.

BOB: I suppose a lot of it depends on who you're talking with.

COACH: Yes, it always depends on the audience, you're right. And the atmosphere. You've got to know what game you're in or concerto or play so that you communicate with the appropriate style. In the theatre, style is knowing what play you're in.

KNOWING WHAT PLAY YOU'RE IN

BOB: *(smiling, knowingly)* You're not going to be very successful if you're playing a different game.

COACH: Right.

BOB: Maybe that's a big part of what I'm feeling here in trying to address the highest level *(moving back to his diagram on the whiteboard).* I don't know that I understand what kind of game they're playing up there *(circling the highest level box in red).* At first glance it seems like I should be able to do what I do, play the actions I naturally play, and everything will be fine. *(with some exasperation)* But when I look at the situation I'm not sure of the rules or the score or the script you were talking about. I don't know what game I'm playing and how I fit in.

COACH: It's good to get some feedback about how you're acting, isn't it?

BOB: Yeah, and I have to a point, but it would be helpful to see if some of my actions are impacting people the way I think they are.

IMPACTING YOUR AUDIENCE

COACH: Until you know that, you'll probably lack confidence as so many actors do when they perform. There are a few weeks of rehearsal where you have the director, stage manager, and fellow actors responding to what you do. And soon they know what's coming and pretty much what you'll do so they naturally stop responding to what you're doing in rehearsal. Then you approach dress rehearsals when all the technical things start happening and there's another audience that you count on for feedback--designers, costumers, crew members, follow-spot operator. And they see your stuff and respond for a little while and yet they've got a job to do so their focus is split and they stop reacting to what you're doing.

BOB: I bet that's tough when you're getting no response to your stuff, especially the funny parts.

COACH: Or the parts that are supposed to be funny.

BOB: Wow, that's brutal!

COACH: Yeah no kidding. Then you've got preview audiences if you're lucky, who are friends of the theatre usually, and know they're in for some pretty bumpy performances. In fact they kind of like to see the scenery not work, you go up on your lines or the button pop off a costume. They get to see the whole play and give you even better feedback and are usually pretty enthusiastic. But as you get to opening night and the critics out there, you start to play actions outside of what you're doing in the play. You want to make a good impression--talk about wanting to impress-- because you'd love to have a good review to send home and you want more people to see the thing you've been working on. So the pressure goes up and the confidence can take a huge blow. Tension enters into your performance 'cause you're so wrapped up with what the audience thinks rather than what's going on in the story you're trying to tell. More science than art usually.

(Bob has drifted around to the back of his chair, leaning on it with both hands)

BOB: The audience is where your head is.

COACH: Exactly! And they see the pressure and often the anxiety around your performance.

GET TO KNOW YOUR AUDIENCE – WHAT DO THEY WANT?

BOB: *(spinning his chair slowly, with a distant look)* So I best get a handle on who's watching and watch them to see how they act.

COACH: Yeah, that's great. One senior executive I work with talks about "sizing up" her audience. She's got great presence and makes eye contact with what seems like everyone. She genuinely enjoys talking with a large audience, but what she's really doing is reading their energy, if you will, by noticing what they're giving her while she's talking. She said it usually happens for her in the first couple minutes of her talk. Now, she can do this because she really knows her material.

BOB: Sounds like it.

COACH: First and foremost you've got to get to know the audience so you can really focus your performance on helping them get what they want.

BOB: That's what you do in the theatre?

COACH: Well, we're presumptuous enough to think we're preparing something that thousands of people are going to like and be engaged in! That's the director's job mostly but everyone has a sense of it. We imagine an audience who will like this joke, that sight gag, this provocative question, or this moment of high emotion as they journey through the play. We predict their response, but only learn their true reaction in the moments of performance.

BOB: Ah! *(stopping the spinning chair)* So, even though you have rehearsed and know exactly what you're going to say and do and what happens when, you don't really know what's going to happen until the audience responds.

COACH: Yes, that's exactly right! And so we spend a lot of time creating what we call the "illusion of the first time". It's like we've never done what we are doing before this exact moment. I'll tell you, an audience can sniff out a stale performance faster than something rotting in the trash. They never want to see last night's performance.

BOB: Yes, I see! *(jotting down a thought in his notebook)*

COACH: Hey, on Broadway, everyone knows it's opening night. But for a leader there's no latitude. You're expected to be on whatever the day.

BOB: Or night. *(moving quickly to sit back down on the edge of his chair, with focused energy)* Maybe this is getting at what I'm feeling about this audience. I'm trying to predict what they're going to say or do, and I'm guessing at their response and that's freaking me out a bit so my confidence goes down.

COACH: Which is understandable.

BOB: But if I prepare as best I can, and hit the stage going for it, and experience their reaction there and then, then I've got a better chance of engaging with them.

COACH: You've hit the nail on the head, Bob. *Prepare* is the key word I heard. So what goes into good preparation? Perhaps... *(draws another box on the quickly crowding whiteboard)*:

Preparation
Know your lines
Know the setting
Know your tools
Anticipate questions
Be ready to change
Believe and Enjoy!

...a list to start with so that you can have the great qualities we look to in our leaders, like:

Desired qualities
Refreshed
Organized
Logical
On point
Adaptable
Entertaining

BOB: "Ready to change" so that I can appear adaptable is where I'd like to get. It can be fairly volatile out there sometimes.

COACH: You never know how many interactions your audience has been in that day. You don't know where they came from just before your time with them. They may have just received terrible or fantastic news on the phone as they sat down to listen to you. What you can bring is freshness--write that down as one of your actions, to 'refresh' or 'freshen'--to a pretty uninteresting day.

BOB: So few people do this!

COACH: *(continuing as Bob adds to his list)* That in itself adds to your overall positive dynamic and helps your message have impact. It's getting to know them-- specifically, what they *want* as an audience--that can help you really hit the mark. To do that though, you've got to spend time looking at things from their perspective which is really challenging since we tend to be wrapped up in "us" when we go to develop the content of our message.

BOB: *(assuring, with no doubt)* I can do it though.

COACH: I'm sure you can, Bob! It's starting off by swinging the camera around to *their* perspective that's critical. If you figure out what they want you're well on your way to helping them get it! And if they can help you get what you want, they're much more invested in the outcome of what's happening between you and them.

BOB: *(cautioning)* Sounds easy enough, but that's not the reality of the situation. Getting to know them is harder than it sounds. That's what I was talking about earlier--I don't know the game I'm in and the players are tough to figure out.

COACH: Like a great actor, you've got to be a great observer of people, of life. Then you've got to take a stab at figuring out what people want in the situation you're in. One leader I worked with just wanted to help their team succeed. They wanted to take action--pick up the phone, talk to their boss, get more money. They wanted to move obstacles from their team's path so everyone could move forward. It was incredibly frustrating for that leader when people would come to them without the action part figured out. Inform?

Forget it! Educate? Sometimes, but for this leader you need to let them know what you want them to <u>do</u> to help you.

BOB: Well that's just one example. Everyone may want something slightly different. And when you go to talk to a team, forget it! *(flopping back in his chair, hands behind his head with elbows out to the side)* You're fighting a political and personality battle then.

COACH: All the more reason to find out, somehow, as much as you can about them. Ask, 'What does this audience want from me at this time?' And ask them, as appropriate. If you don't ask or at least invest some time in figuring this out you'll tend to prepare based on interactions of the past. And this prejudgment thing can really get in the way.

PREJUDGING YOUR AUDIENCE

BOB: Not too long ago I went into my VP's office thinking she would respond in a certain way because of all this stuff I heard about her. Turned out that some of it was true and she responded the way I thought but other stuff I heard was way wrong. I nearly blew it!

COACH: I've known actors who would deliver their performance based on the day of the week.

BOB: You're kidding.

COACH: I wish I were. In fact one actor who has gone on to a major TV role and some fame would walk into our dressing room we shared and say, "All right! Now what day of the week is it?"

BOB: I still don't see how that would make a difference.

COACH: Well, depending on the day of the week, audiences tend to have certain characteristics. So the actor would base their performance on their take on the characteristics of the audience on that particular day. Tuesday night was the cheap audience, Wednesday are the people who don't go to church, Thursday night they're young and cheap, Friday night is the party crowd, Saturday night they're fat and drunk, and Sunday are the blue hairs.

BOB: What about Monday?

COACH: We're off on Monday.

BOB: Wow!

COACH: Yeah, amazing isn't it. So what?

BOB: What do you mean, "so what?"

COACH: What was the "wow" about?

BOB: *(smiling incredulously)* Well, to think that someone could have such a limited view of an entire audience! I mean, there are probably several hundred people in each crowd and you can't just put them all into the category of "blue hairs" and expect to reach them all.

COACH: And, the possibility....

BOB: *(on a roll)* Sorry to interrupt you but the "and" is, I would guess that the actor's performance would be stale. They'd be playing to another crowd when they first saw blue hairs out there and from then on they treat the...what was it, Sunday when the blue hairs attend?

COACH: Yes, Sunday.

BOB: So each Sunday crowd gets the ol' blue hair treatment!

COACH: Yes, that's certainly part of the trap. *(drawing on the board while he talks)*

Traps - Audience
Treat every audience the same way
Let your material stay the same
No change in your performance
You were successful the last time

COACH: *(continued)* Suppose you treated every senior executive team the same way just because they're "senior leaders". Would that work?

BOB: No, I don't think so.

COACH: And think about times when you have to give the same talk over and again. It's the same material. You know what you're going to say, you dress basically the same, use the same presentation. What really changes in your performance?

BOB: The audience.

ADAPTING TO YOUR AUDIENCE

COACH: There ya go. If they change you'd better be ready to change too! And you may change some. Maybe you don't feel like being energetic in front of that audience of engineers. Perhaps you've lost some belief in your content due to the way things have gone organizationally the day before. You best dive into your bag of technique, your repertoire, your structure of action and be ready to play no matter how you or they respond. What if you have that big joke coming up, a key moment of fun for everyone, and no one laughs?

(pause)

BOB: I don't know what I'd do.

COACH: You'd be ready to go on with the show, right?

BOB: I'd have to.

COACH: So I've been drawing here for awhile. How about you draw out what's in your bag of tricks that you've discovered from our discussion so far?

(Bob takes the marker and draws as he talks)

BOB: Well, I'd have to say know my audience, play the right action from a list I develop, try to interact often with my audience and change as much as the situation requires. And when I'm ready, like I'm starting to feel right now, go for it and quit fearing so damn much.

Bob's Bag of Tricks
Know my audience
Play the right action from my list
Interact with my audience
Change as the situation requires
Go for it when ready

COACH: Yeah, just go for it! There's a time when you must go on stage when there's no turning back. And to be ready to play in that space means you understand something, hopefully a lot, about your audience, the atmosphere surrounding the situation, your structure of action, and as an actor you're set with costume, make-up, and the right energy to <u>go</u> <u>on</u>.

BOB: That's what I'm talking about when I say go for it. I just say it in fewer words.

ACHIEVING A STATE OF DISCOVERY

COACH: *(enjoying this)* Got it! And if you're ready to go for it, you're ready for the greatest state to be in as a performer--a state of discovery with yourself and for your audience.

BOB: A state of discovery--so I'm ready to discover something?

COACH: Maybe a new perspective on what you've already prepared. A new sense from the audience that you didn't know was there. A new point of humor. Or pain. Something that makes what you're performing better than before, or sends you back to the drawing board with renewed energy, or causes you to scrap your original idea all together.

BOB: Discovery.

COACH: Right.

(pause, Bob is writing a note)

BOB: Feels nervous.

COACH: It's being out there on the edge.

BOB: *(testing with a slight smile)* And that's supposed to make me feel good or something?

COACH: It may make you feel uncomfortable. And that isn't necessarily a bad thing. You'll have your homework done. And you'll have a structure of action to play out. Structure brings freedom. The freedom to discover.

BOB: *(challenging)* I don't get the uncomfortable part. I want and try to feel comfortable when I interact at the next levels. I work to feel confident. Now you're saying that I should feel discomfort? That really goes against my instincts and what I've tried to practice for quite awhile now.

EMBRACING DISCOMFORT AND CONFLICT

COACH: Most people may respond the same way I would guess. They want comfort in what they're doing. But being comfortable seems contrary to the work dynamic.

BOB: Well I'm not saying that we should be totally comfortable in our work, but some degree of comfort is nice.

COACH: It strikes me that a comfortable environment might be less conducive to generating effective actions.

BOB: *(pushing)* Meaning that if I'm more comfortable I'm less active?

USING CREATIVE TENSION AND CONFLICT

COACH: In a sense I think that may be. Call it creative tension. It's the energy that's held taut between actor and audience. The thing that makes us stay there to watch the play and doesn't let us go. We almost don't want it to end--we enjoy getting wrapped up in it. And as theatre artists, we sustain the creative tension by building conflict or discomfort into what we do.

BOB: That sounds contrary to what we do in business.

COACH: You're all about reducing conflict.

BOB: Yeah, pretty much.

COACH: And that's very active in itself. But maybe there's some relief in thinking that the discomfort we feel in our interactions is something that benefits our performance. Rather than getting caught up in how challenging, or stressful an interaction is...

BOB: *(up out of chair, crossing to window, looking out)*...like my interaction with the senior leaders...

COACH: ...we put another thought in there. What if we actually thought that the conflict helps us create a better structure of action?

BOB: *(turning back to the coach, grabbing a squishy ball to play with)* So the conflict I'm noticing and experiencing actually helps me?

COACH: *(relaxing back in his chair)* I think it may help you when you engage at the senior level. You said that you don't know how to play the game at that level—some days I'm not sure anybody really knows how to play the game--and the gap between where you are as rookie, if you will, and where you want to be causes conflict. So, you've got a couple choices it seems. You can move away from the conflict or you can embrace it.

BOB: *(tossing the ball in the air and catching it)* I don't really have a choice in the matter.

COACH: Don't you?

(Bob continues the toss and catch)

BOB: No, if I want to keep my job I embrace it.

COACH: Is that what you see happening with people around you?

BOB: For the most part, yes.

COACH: Do you notice people who seem to stay on the outside of conflict?

BOB: Yes, some. I see those who actively avoid it and some who minimize it. Some are just passive—they don't do much it appears.

COACH: How active would you say they are?

BOB: Actually they tend to be very inactive, those who pull away from the conflict.

COACH: Would they tend to be in the higher paid or lower paid positions?

BOB: Lower paid.

COACH: More perks?

BOB: Less, definitely.

COACH: Promotable? High performers?

BOB: I don't think of them as promotable. I see them, and it may just be my thing, as functional, competent, doing their job.

COACH: What about you?

BOB: *(apparently more interested in squishing the ball)* I think I tend to embrace conflict.

COACH: You are in the position you're in for a reason, yes?

BOB: Yeah, I guess so. I do think I go after things pretty strongly. *(stops squishing)* But it doesn't make me any more confident and comfortable. In fact the anxiety is higher when I go to engage and work through the conflict.

COACH: *(taking a note)* So the greater the conflict the more you engage.

BOB: Yes I think so. But the anxiety increases.

COACH: That's why I think it might help to try a different mindset within your goal of playing at the upper level. *(stands, pacing a bit to and from the whiteboard, around back of his chair)* What if you were to start thinking of conflict as a good thing? What if in your structure of action you persisted with actions that leverage conflict?

BOB: You mean like accepting the anxiety I feel as a thing I should look forward to?

COACH: Perhaps. *(leaning against the wall by the door, matching Bob's apparent nonchalance)* Actors consciously build conflict into their structure of action. Playwrights definitely create obstacles for their actors to work through. Have you ever noticed how things may be going swimmingly in a movie--the characters are "comfortable". They're managing along well for maybe the first fifteen minutes or so.

BOB: You know something bad is going to happen.

COACH: Or seemingly good.

BOB: Right. Though that can be a source of conflict as well, especially in a comedy.

COACH: Yes, a comedy is filled with conflict! Seems like the harder someone tries to get through a conflict the funnier it can be. It's the basis for comedy from Shakespeare to sitcoms. So, *(pressing)* why do you think that happens?

BOB: What, the moment when something changes for the better or worse? Well *(stating the obvious)* it wouldn't be a very interesting story without some bumps in the road! It certainly makes things more interesting.

COACH: So the audience gets more engaged would you say?

BOB: Yes. *(growing impatience)*

COACH: *(not giving in)* So the built-in conflict, the conflict purposefully created resulted in a more engaging experience.

BOB: Right.

COACH: It's also much more engaging for the actors. You've got to give us something to work against for the drama to come out, whether comedy or tragedy. If you don't, as a playwright or director I'll manufacture conflict so that I have something to work against. I notice this in cats, too.

BOB: *(a bit bewildered though a cat fan)* Cats?

COACH: Cats are excellent at building conflict into their play. They'll grab a toy in their mouth, walk around with it and then put it under a chair *(using his chair as an example)* or in a box--somewhere that makes it harder to get. Then they have to struggle more to get it. I guess it's more fun that way.

BOB: It's a little bizarre thinking about cats when trying to get to the next level but I can see your point I think. *(smiling with some impatience)* And, what the hell. It seems fairly natural if cats are doing it too!

COACH: *(summing up to move forward)* Many people don't seek out challenges so they're less active. Others do and are more active. The trick is to learn to appreciate conflict as a way of improving your structure of action--the actions you play, and the efficiency and effectiveness of how you get things done. And along the way you may just have some fun.

BOB: *(still dodging, kneading the squishy ball now back and forth between his hands)* I have enough conflict to deal with. I can't see building more into my day!

COACH: *(heading back to sit down)* For you then, trying to appreciate conflict as a way to more effective actions may be enough. For others, they may need more conflict to bring out their best work.

(pause, Bob takes this in)

PURPOSEFUL CONFLICT

BOB: *(slowly, as he works it out)* I can see how that might work for my team. I'm all for them being more effective and engaged, and from what you've said I could see how they can benefit from some more conflict. Purposeful conflict. That has some interesting things about it. I think I already help in that area. Not that I'm a source of conflict I hope, but that the projects and assignments I give them help them stretch beyond their comfort zone.

COACH: Interesting.

BOB: Which I think is great for their growth. *(getting re-engaged)* Now some of them call it piling on work I think and I'm not sure how I'll explain actions and conflict like we've discussed, but now that I think of it, I do see a difference in their actions when they've got a job with new or more conflict around it. Some buckle, some embrace as you said, and some completely break under the pressure of conflict. But they all have to do something differently to address the conflict.

COACH: You sound like a director with your team of actors.

BOB: *(tossing the ball to the Coach)* Actually it's a lot like that I imagine. Except for that actors are involved in a fiction and this is real life.

COACH: *(catching the ball then slowly placing it in the middle of the table between them, laughing)* Don't tell actors that! It's true though. We're talking about people providing for themselves and their families here.

BOB: *(sitting)* But I can see how they can do that better by thinking about this. They can be more engaged, more in control, more purposeful in their work. To think that we're talking about building more conflict into our work is out there for me I gotta say! Even a cat has a limit to the conflict they can take. If there's not enough they get bored and leave the toy and if there's too much they leave too.

COACH: I've noticed that about my cats. If I jump into the game and play it too vigorously they get mad at me and leave.

BOB: They often look very insulted about the whole thing.

COACH: Yes. It's almost like they're saying, "It wasn't my idea for you to play that way."

BOB: Which is probably a pretty good point here. The conflict has to be appropriate to the game, a play as you would say, so that one doesn't leave but stays in there with new action.

COACH: *(writing fast in his notebook)* Great point! There's appropriateness to all of this and it may take some investment of risk before you understand the appropriateness of the conflict. The conflict will lead to action, which also may or may not be appropriate. And you'll feel that--you or others--and adjust accordingly. What you risk is not getting to new action. You do the same as you've always done and expected and let the anxiety caused by conflict get the best of you. In short, you don't change. There's little growth and improvement there and probably won't allow you to lead as effectively at the next level.

BOB: Let me see if I get this, because I want to share this with my group. You ought to write a book about this and make my job easier.

COACH: All right.

BOB: *(checking his notes)* First, I want to try thinking about conflict differently, as a source of better action. Then, I want to consciously build in conflict and leverage it so that better actions emerge, and so that we all are more engaged.

Bob's Bag of Tricks – Conflict!
Think about conflict differently
Conflict as a source of new action
Consciously build in purposeful conflict as appropriate
Leverage conflict to improve actions
All are more engaged

COACH: Yes, exactly, and if I may add, playing selected actions can enhance the conflict, making it more impactful for everyone involved.

BOB: *(using his new list of actions)* So if I challenge, confront, stir-up, question, provoke even, the conflict will be heightened?

COACH: Yes, and remember that actions are always focused on reaching immediate goals that lead to your overall goal, what you want in life. So in business we're always focused on what the business objectives are and how we move the business forward. If we act outside of that, well, we're in the wrong play.

BOB: The wrong business.

COACH: Yes.

WHEN YOU'RE IN A BAD PLAY

BOB: *(leaning back in chair, crossing arms)* So let's say you're in a play that you know is no good.

COACH: What do you mean?

BOB: Well let's say that you're in the play, you're definitely a performer, and you've got this feeling that what you're playing just isn't very good.

COACH: So there's a bad script.

BOB: A bad script, story--it just doesn't feel like it's going to work.

COACH: Sounds like you've got a choice. You can stay in the play and make the best of it or you can bail out.

BOB: But if you bail you'll probably leave the rest of the group high and dry.

COACH: Well, it depends on where you are in the production process. Earlier on they can get a replacement. Later on and your understudy may take the role. Either way you've thrown a big wrench in the works.

BOB: *(getting it out, reluctantly)* I'm thinking there's something wrong with the play I'm working on. I've done my research, partnered with some people, have a recommendation ready, but I've got this gut feeling that this isn't the right thing to do. I think the idea is good but with our business I don't think it will really move us forward.

COACH: Then say so. Tell the rest of the team that it's not making sense to you.

BOB: *(pressured exasperation)* But I was brought in to make this happen! It was handed down to me to finish the thing.

COACH: *(playing Bob's mind for a moment)* But you're thinking this isn't going to work and it's your duty to let the rest of the team know that this isn't in the best interest of the greater cause--the customers you have, the shareholders you keep happy, right?

(the challenge and resulting energy builds...)

BOB: But the show must go on.

COACH: It doesn't have to go on with you in your role.

BOB: But I'll never be cast again if I'm not careful.

COACH: I can see that. You want to work again in the next production?

BOB: Yes, I'd like to reach the highest level I can, and I'm afraid if I speak my mind on this I may not get there.

SERVING TWO AUDIENCES - COLLABORATION

COACH: *(recognizing the conflict, with passion and confrontation)* You're serving a couple of audiences here and you've got a tough choice to make. Which audience do you want to satisfy? Ultimately it seems that your whole production--cast, crew and operations support--would want to satisfy paying customers whose butts fill the seats. However, I understand when the other audience, your management, sees it another way. There's a discrepancy between what they see as the imperative and what you see customers wanting. Figuring out the right audience to serve is critical to the effectiveness of your performance.

BOB: No kidding.

COACH: It's like the give and take relationship between the producer of the theatre and the director they hire for each show. Every party is supposed to have the best interest of the paying audience in mind. Yet each may have a different picture in their head of what the performance should be like. They each presume to know what the collective audience will like most about the play--perhaps in your case, the final product. Hopefully they learn over time to collaborate and develop a level of trust that allows a freedom of expression with each other. They match up well by sharing similar artistic sensibilities, and in order to work with each other they probably have seen something they like in each other's work. But they don't always agree on the best interpretation of the play for the audience at that theatre. They reach agreement on when, for example, the producer can come and view a rehearsal. The director and actors want the producer to be comfortable with what's going on in the telling of the story, to a point. The producer may disagree with some of the very personal and artistically sensitive things that the director and actors have put together. Yet it is their *duty* to speak out if their paying customers would take offense at something in the play, or if something integral to the playwright's story is being misrepresented. And the director should speak up if they think the story--its central theme, idea, and value--is being compromised by an over-controlling producer. Yet in the end, all have the same objective in mind--a stimulating theatrical event that takes an audience to another place for a time and brings them back understanding more about themselves than before.

BOB: I can see how that works--a very tricky artistic, collaborative relationship between the team members.

COACH: *(refocusing)* Like in your business.

BOB: I don't know about the artistic part. I guess it's got some of the same finesse points.

COACH: I just worked with a client who is still regretting not speaking out about a product their company was producing that just didn't make financial sense.

BOB: Why didn't they talk?

COACH: *(raising his voice authoritatively)* Because the CEO and COO wanted this product done and out there! My client was told by their boss to get it done or take a hike.

BOB: Serving two audiences *(another note in his book)*.

COACH: And all together, the company ended up spending about a quarter million dollars *per customer* to get them on board of the few customers they had! Think you'd get some decent margin off of that? How about the cost of severance packages when the product failed? And the impact on the remaining employees at the company?

BOB: Because someone didn't speak up. And wanted to satisfy the next level.

COACH: The next, next, *next* level.

BOB: There's similar finesse in what you described with the theatre production scenario. But there's more of a directive approach here. *(growing intensity)* I've got a business objective that says a certain amount of new dollars will come in and it's part of our forecast of what business we'll do. So there's little room for creative collaboration around that.

COACH: *(prodding)* No changes allowed in your forecasts? You drive to the goal no matter what happens or changes?

BOB: It's "get it done" regardless of the challenge or the change.

COACH: Even if the challenge you face impacts the very increase in dollars that you're trying to achieve?

(silence)

COACH: Even if the audience that pays the dollars you forecast isn't going to want what you have to offer?

BOB: Hmm.

BEING IN TWO PLAYS AT ONCE

COACH: You're in two plays here. One is a political story where the audience knows politics and plays politics well. The other is a story of a life of a customer made better by what you have to sell them. I've never seen an actor who can be in two plays at once. Now maybe there's a compromise, but you've got to figure out which is going to get most of your attention right now. *(louder, pushing)* You've got to choose, Bob! What's the right thing to do? Cover your ass and deliver something that will end up losing money?! That may satisfy one audience for awhile. Insist on excellence and quality for your paying customers by not insulting them with something they don't want and doesn't work? That will be better for them now and down the road, but someone may kick your ass now for that one. A classic actor and director battle! Through rehearsal they both advance their vision with trial and error. They create an environment where they can duke it out without killing each other! As rehearsal goes on the best actors push the limits of story possibilities-- they push hard! They test the dynamics of the character and story believability. They do this to find the best way of telling the story. The best directors help to edit their choices and assist when they're stuck. And they make sure that the story points are clear and the action is believable. BUT BOTH THE DIRECTOR AND ACTOR HAVE THE RESPONSIBILITY TO STOP REHEARSAL IF THE PRODUCTION IS HEADING IN THE WRONG DIRECTION! They risk their jobs to honor the audience, the playwright, the theatre, and themselves.

BOB: *(calmly)* What if they get down the road a bit and realize they have a bad play?

COACH: Back to your original question--sorry.

BOB: That's okay.

COACH: Even the very best actors can't make a bad play good. The reviews from the critics in a production like that go, "Fine performances from accomplished actors but what a waste on this play." You can play compelling actions all over the place and yet something just doesn't click with the audience--the PAYING audience. The story just doesn't come together to make sense.

BOB: That's what I'm feeling right now.

COACH: So you have to decide. Customers? Bosses? The right play? Not a good role for me? Some compromise? My integrity? Whatever you decide you're going to have to address the upper management audience and for that your structure of action will come in handy.

APPLYING YOUR STRUCTURE OF ACTION

BOB: *(focusing in)* Yeah, let's think about that some more. So, my objective in life is to lead an organization like the one I'm in now, my immediate objective or want, as you said...that changes, right?

COACH: Yes, usually scene-by-scene but it may change within a scene as well.

BOB: Right. So to use the chart on actions, my immediate objective in this scene, what I want to accomplish right now is … to do the right thing for our customers.

COACH: Okay.

BOB: And so there's a scene I have to play out with my boss, and soon.

COACH: Really?

BOB: Yeah, so I better figure out what actions I'm going to play, yes?

COACH: Yes!

BOB: Well, I'll have to ease into the situation.

COACH: So are you easing in your boss?

BOB: I'm easing into the situation.

COACH: So what are you doing to your boss while easing in--coaxing, prepping, guiding?

BOB: Oh yes, I'm to play actions toward someone.

COACH: Right.

BOB: *(a bit flustered)* I'm...you're much better at these actions than I am.

COACH: *(encouraging)* It takes some practice.

BOB: *(determined)* I'll get it. I like it!

COACH: Great!

BOB: *(clicking now)* I'll take coax for now, and throw in a little guiding. Then I'll have to confront without shocking her at some point. And I've got to assure her that everything will work out fine. I may have to challenge her thinking. "Alert" may be something I have to do, you know, to open her eyes. And I may surprise her by accident.

COACH: So not intentionally surprise...

BOB: No. But it may happen.

COACH: *(looking at his list)* What I've heard so far then is coax, guide, confront, assure, challenge, alert, surprise. Is that your list?

BOB: I really may have to convince through justification with data. So that may come up, too.

COACH: Adding convince to your list. What else?

BOB: I think that's a good list to start with.

Bob's Structure of Action - Conversation with Boss

Action	Immediate Want	Overall Want
Coax Guide Confront Assure Challenge Alert Surprise Convince	Do the right thing for customers	Lead an organization like the one I'm in now

IMPROVISING

COACH: So are you ready to abandon your whole plan of action?

BOB: What?

COACH: You walk into your boss's office ready to play out your script and your boss responds in a way that you don't expect. Are you ready to change your approach?

BOB: I don't know. I guess I'd need some different actions.

COACH: You may. Or your might need to be flexible in what you do and when. That's what play is all about. You build up this repertoire of actions and you go in to the scene ready to convince and that doesn't achieve the desired result so you try different tactics.

BOB: *(clarifying)* Different actions.

COACH: Yes, we sometimes call actions "tactics" or "intentions". As long as you're not getting what you want you change actions until your objectives are met.

BOB: And my objectives can change too?

COACH: Yes, as appropriate. On changing actions, I remember visiting my niece when she was three years old. She was playing in her room. I was in the next room reading and my sister was in the room next to me doing some work. My niece wanted my sister for something and called out, "Mom." My sister must not have heard her because she didn't answer. So after a few seconds my niece called out "Mom" again with a little different energy. Still no answer. So with more energy "Mom" was called out a third time. And a fourth. And a fifth. Each with slightly different energy and subtly different in action as the situation became more urgent. I was fascinated by the change in each more critically expressed call of "Mom". Seventeen times she said "Mom" and each one was unique. Why? Because my niece wasn't getting what she wanted so she changed the action seventeen times to try again. And she's doing this naturally at three years old.

BOB: If this is so natural, why work at it? Why coach around this?

DISCIPLINE OF ACTION

COACH: *(slight smile, direct)* Because you brought it up.

BOB: *(taken aback)* You mean due to that one word "worry" we're down the road here about 45 minutes?

COACH: *(testing)* I just want to be sure that...if you see this discipline of action working for you....

BOB: *(impatiently)* I do see it or we'd be talking about something else. *(refocusing)* Discipline of action you said.

COACH: Yes, discipline.

BOB: So it's a discipline.

COACH: Yes, in that you have to exert energy to apply it and keep it going.

BOB: Like anything else I suppose.

COACH: It takes attention, and as for your question about why coach around this, yes, it is natural, instinctive, but often our personality or environment, learning, even a strong emotional response to something can throw us off the accurate action track. It's often that something has gone wrong in a situation, and after dissecting it a bit we realize that there was a mistake in the action being played.

BOB: *(back with the Coach, affirming)* I know what you're saying. When I get too emotional I can say or do stuff I don't mean.

COACH: And we all experience that. When we do that we're not as effective in the roles we play. Often it's the slightest degree of inflection in what we say that causes an unwanted reaction in our audience. We need to realize that the slight shifts in actions we play can have huge impact on our message. So we continue to subtly shape the appropriateness of the actions we play to best get what we want.

CHOOSING THE APPROPRIATE ACTION

BOB: So the challenge is in the nuance of action, getting just the right one to be most effective.

COACH: *(redirecting)* I wouldn't want anyone to get hung up on something like "Oh I've got to have just the right action here before I do anything."

BOB: That could trap someone into doing nothing.

COACH: Right. It's more to consider the slight changes you naturally make and can effectively put to use in your interactions. I'm working with a client who has been described as going into "attack mode". At the core of that state of being is the action "to attack". If you think about action as being directed at someone else, how effective do you think this person will be in getting what they want?

BOB: Well if they're attacking people I don't think they'll be very effective.

COACH: Probably not.

BOB: It might feel good to do that or get it out which may be helpful for that person, but they're limited when they try to work with people to get what they want.

COACH: So what should they do?

BOB: *(jabbing)* Not attack!

COACH: *(jabbing back)* What should they do instead? Before you answer that you should understand that this person is highly regarded by managers, peers, the team they manage, largely for their passion, drive, directness, and the results they deliver.

BOB: Wow, when you say that it changes the situation.

COACH: *(pressing)* And those around them have said that if this person loses that productive energy by adjusting their style, then it wouldn't be worth it to change.

BOB: *(unbelieving, up on his feet)* So they like the passion and want that to continue but don't like the attack part which can be fueled by strong passion!

COACH: You got it.

BOB: *(circling to the white board, turning back to the coach)* So what do they do you asked?

COACH: Yes. Or if you were my client, the "Attacker", what would you do?

BOB: *(dismissing)* Find a new job.

COACH: That's an option.

BOB: *(direct, serious)* With another company.

COACH: *(thinking of a better solution)* Hmm.

BOB: Where they love the attack mode.

COACH: Other options? I mean this is a very valuable leader in this company.

BOB: Back off on attack.

COACH: Back off to what?

BOB: Something not as strong. *(big smile)* Oh, I see where you're going! Back off to a more appropriate action *(back to his notes)*.

COACH: There you go!

BOB: *(pointing in his book)* Like challenge. You can challenge without attacking. Or confront. Or startle, surprise, push off guard, tempt...

COACH: Tempt?

BOB: Yeah. You could draw them into your point of view.

COACH: In a workshop with marketers the other day someone said they seduce.

BOB: Bet that shocked the group!

COACH: Yes, they laughed and gasped a bit.

BOB: *(sitting)* I can see why.

COACH: And then he said, "I really do seduce. I write stuff that seduces customers into buying our services." And though the others were still somewhat uncomfortable, they quieted and thought about it---that this guy wasn't a pervert but someone who has a good idea of what they really do to people day-to-day.

TURNING ACTIONS INTO ROLES

BOB: They had to say what they do out loud?

COACH: Yes. In the workshop they were working on how they communicate the value they bring to customers. So we took a look at the actions they currently play to do that. Each person worked with another to list the actions they play and then chose one that best described what they really do. Then we went around the room and heard each person say, "I _____," filling in the blank with the action they chose.

BOB: How'd they respond?

COACH: They were quiet, and engaged. We started hearing through each person a pure, simple description of what a group *actually does*; what they really do irrespective of mission statements, business goals, marketing-ease, processes, systems--what they really do to people at work and their customers.

BOB: *(confirming)* You just heard the actions they play.

COACH: Yes, and then they more clearly defined their roles since, as we touched on earlier, all they have to do is add an "er" or "or" to their action and they have their role.

BOB: So seduce becomes Seducer. To tempt becomes Tempter. What a way to get a nickname!

COACH: Yes, you can have some fun with this. And define the real role you play or want to play going forward.

BOB: *(writing)* Your theme!

COACH: Your core action or role.

BOB: *(leaning in, quietly intense)* So with this Attacker you mention. They're putting people off with that performance.

COACH: And limiting their opportunity for advancement. That's from their VP, not me. She called me in to work with him.

BOB: *(challenging)* But people they work with like that energy sometimes. This person gets the job done when others can't.

COACH: Yes, they value that part of them.

BOB: So that action is appropriate at times.

COACH: For the right audience in the right atmosphere.

BOB: They have to be aware when they're acting this out.

PROCESS OF IMPROVING YOUR ACTING

COACH: Awareness is the first step. In actor training, awareness is where we spend a ton of time, opening people up to what they're doing, thinking, and feeling.

BOB: So our Attacker has to be aware when they're in that mode.

COACH: Which can be tricky since that action may come out when they're least thinking about it--when they're tired, stressed, or emotional. But only if they're aware of it can they go to work on it.

BOB: *(thinking about his own situation)* Sounds like careful work that takes some time.

COACH: It is.

BOB: *(pressured)* And time is what I'm short on! That's what really gets me about this kind of thing. It takes time to really go to work on this and I feel jammed as it is.

COACH: I understand how you feel. Let's step back for a second and review the process we've discussed today. This may be what it looks like, you tell me. *(makes some room on the whiteboard)* Ok, so I'm going at this as a performer, an actor in whatever situation. I've got stuff I do before the show, during, and then after. If I'm tight on time I need a tight structure like:

Pre-Performance	Performance	Post-Performance
Structure action Practice Prepare tools	Play actions Adapt actions Discover	Get feedback Change for next performance

COACH: *(continued)* This helps me address those times when I feel hurried trying to get everything done. I'm finding though, with work and at home, if I invest time up front on an issue and really work to figure out what's going on--planning the action of the thing--I can usually get it turned around and save time from fixing it again and again down the road. But first I've got to be aware of what's happening and then break it down into the sequence of events--in theatrical or story terms, the plot that led up to the issue.

BOB: Got it. The Attacker needs to know that they're attacking, then step back and figure out what led up to it.

COACH: Yes, and once you do that you can focus on the plot points that caused you to play the wrong action...

BOB: For that situation.

COACH: ...exactly, and then go to work on the single events you can control and manage--really do something about. Too often we get the direction from someone that we're "attacking and really need to stop it" but have no idea why it's happening and are clueless about how to fix it. Breaking it down into plot points lets us manage one action at a time.

BOB: *(confirming in his notes)* Like you said earlier where a good actor changes actions frequently depending on the scene to keep it interesting and move the story forward.

COACH: Hamlet and Ophelia are especially challenging. Read what he says to her and you wonder why he says it. What did she do to him?! What happened between them? It's very challenging to understand why he's treating her as he does. All we have to go on is what he says--very little is described as to what he does. Suppose you decide in playing Hamlet that you're angry with Ophelia and therefore "pummel" her for the rest of the scene. That could make sense for a while but it wouldn't be very compelling for the whole scene. And just think if you treated your team here at work that way for awhile? How would that go over? Your audience would have you figured out pretty fast and lose interest.

TAKING RISKS WITH ACTIONS

BOB: *(doubting)* My audience may tend to lose interest in me.

COACH: *(probing)* Meaning?

BOB: They may figure out where I'm going with my "script" and tune me out.

COACH: *(matter of fact)* So change.

BOB: To what?

COACH: What's appropriate for the situation.

BOB: That's what I'm saying--I don't know what's appropriate!

COACH: But you have a list of actions--persuade, guide...

BOB: Titillate. Don't forget titillate.

COACH: And you can play those things.

BOB: Yes. I think I can. I do.

COACH: So switch actions when the conversation isn't going your way.

BOB: When I'm not getting what I want.

COACH: Right. Or your audience isn't getting what they want.

BOB: *(restless)* I guess it's the appropriateness part that's getting me. How do I know what will work, may work, won't offend?

COACH: That's where the risk part comes in *(encouraging)*. You've gotta try it! How do you determine what works in your personal life?

BOB: I just...adapt.

COACH: Are you always successful?

BOB: Of course not.

COACH: Do you ever risk it?

BOB: What?

COACH: The action you play?

BOB: I guess so. Sometimes I really wonder if I should say what I'm about to say and I have to think about that while the conversation is going on.

COACH: And in that moment you're assessing the risk, the impact of what you're about to do to someone.

BOB: I suppose...

COACH: So you make a decision about the action you're going to play. You know the action. Weigh its impact and the risk associated with it, and then you play it.

BOB: Or not. Or pull back.

COACH: Taking on a more appropriate action.

BOB: *(realizing)* Yeah, I would say when you break it down like that, that's pretty much the process. I think I'm getting hung up on the appropriate part.

DETERMINING ALWAYS, SOMETIMES, AND NEVER ACTIONS

COACH: And that's where experience colors your interaction. In the workshops I've conducted on this I ask participants to take on this challenge: I ask them to think about appropriate actions they play at work by selecting actions that they think they should always play, never play, and those that they sometimes have to

play. They complete a chart with the three categories--
Always, Sometimes, and Never:

Always	Sometimes	Never

COACH: *(continued)* Then they share their responses
with the group. It becomes a kind of "how to act" or
"how to behave" guide, and it leads to a sense of the
values they hold and share as a group. Of these
categories, which do you think is the most challenging
for most people to come up with?

BOB: I 'd think they'd be pretty good at getting Never,
and Always should come fairly easy. Sometimes is a
gray area so I'd say that would be the toughest.

COACH: Yes, I agree. Why do you think that's so?

BOB: Because you have to really think about the
situation and what's hard for you to play. And like you
said, the impact that would have on your audience.

COACH: That's where the greatest risk is, too.

BOB: I'm thinking this goes beyond speaking with someone. You have to weigh this out in what you write as well. It's not just spoken, it's written.

ACTION IN WRITING

COACH: How do you see this playing out in your writing?

BOB: The same way as spoken. In fact, I think I've got better insight into this action discipline when I think about my writing.

COACH: How so?

BOB: It seems like I put more time into what I write than what I say out loud. I stop, think about the best way to say something, write it, re-read it, and edit as I go. I don't have that luxury when I speak. Like we discussed earlier, you risk saying what you should or should not say and you have to decide fast which way to go. Like a great improv actor.

COACH: Another role!

BOB: Geez, I'm an improv actor as well! Whether you say it or not, you have the nonverbals that go with it, and they may be out there and noticed by the person you're speaking to before or after you speak.

COACH: *(guiding)* With nonverbals it's like you're communicating things beyond what you actually do or don't say.

BOB: Yes, and then you can send a very different message--a very different action than what you chose to say. *(up on his feet suddenly)* Crap!

COACH: What, we're over time?

BOB: *(to his planner, laptop, paging through his notebook)* No, it's just that the more I think about putting this into practice, the more I wonder how I come across!

PUTTING THE PROCESS INTO PRACTICE

COACH: Oh, yes.

BOB: It's like, *(trying to resist blaming the Coach)* I don't think I'm going to be able to make a move from now on without wondering if I'm on to the right action, communicating the right thing. Maybe if I just sit there, in neutral, everything will be all right!

COACH: *(quietly)* I can understand why you would think that. This, like anything having to do with how we act, is a lot to think about. Remember, we don't want you locking up in inactivity or putting it into neutral! That's inactive. That's boring, which is the biggest crime committed in the theatre and in life, to make things boring! With this, it's awareness first, which is magnified right now because you're focusing on it. Then, with your new awareness, put one or two things into practice. This is the process an actor goes through--awareness, rehearse, perform, evaluate-- always trying new things to get to the right thing, the theatrical truth that supports the story.

BOB: Business truth....

COACH: But eventually, they have to step on stage and go for it. That's what being a professional is all about.

BOB: Right, go for it.

COACH: Even then everything still won't be perfect! So, you get used to your performance, with a bit of practice thrown in, always working on something in front of your audience. It's a bit risky, fresh, and always good, often great. A professional is always good in their performance and often they're great. Bottom line, you forget about your preparation and go for it on stage. The preparation and sense of practice will be there, residually, in your performance while you busy yourself with playing the scene.

BOB: *(re-determined, focusing)* Little by little. Awareness, preparation, practice, performance, all mixed in, forgetting about your self-consciousness and doing it right.

COACH: Exactly. And that takes time, the time you said you had more of when you write something.

BOB: Yes. And like there's a spell-checker in the word processing software, there should be an action-checker.

FINDING ACTION IN YOUR MISSION

COACH: Not a bad idea! I find myself noticing companies' mission statements, or the goals they communicate to the world. I guess, intuitively, I'm an action-checker.

BOB: *(enjoying the obvious)* I'd say you are!

COACH: A new role for me! And what I think about is how the people who work for these companies respond to the action they read in the statements.

BOB: You mean like "to be the best in our field by making customers happy"?

COACH: Yes, that's a good example. "Be the best"--that's a state of being. Go ahead, be the best, RIGHT NOW, DO IT!

BOB: *(bringing it down a notch)* Well, I'd have to know a bit more about how we do that.

COACH: But isn't it clear? If you "make customers happy" you're probably among the best.

BOB: Not necessarily. It doesn't say what I'm supposed to do--there's the action piece--to be the best to make customers happy.

COACH: Right. But that's what goals are for. They tell us how to reach the mission.

BOB: You mean like "grow revenue", "reduce costs"-- that's on everyone's list.

COACH: Those are clearer, but like you said I still don't know what to *do* to people to get there.

BOB: How about "delight customers"?

COACH: Yes, and do I know how to do that? Can you delight me right now? Is delight playable?

BOB: And what different actions might I need to play to get to delight?

COACH: You're sounding like the coach here.

DISCOVERING THE RIGHT ACTION FOR YOUR BUSINESS

BOB: *(enjoying his new awareness)* I'm getting the hang of this! You can engage with a customer, hear them, honor them, encourage, surprise, respect their time, their investment, astound them, serve them--things you'd have on your Always or Sometimes list.

COACH: And that's the stuff people who work for a company--your company--respond to. Grow revenue? DUUUHHH! Manage costs? Double-duh.

BOB: I think people who write those things, myself included, need to look at the actions we choose in writing our guiding principles. Just the word choice is critical to people actually knowing what to do, how to behave. This could be very inspirational to many to listen to this sense of things--how we communicate inside and outside the company.

COACH: It's choosing the right thing to communicate so people truly, intuitively, can respond. So they know how to act.

BOB: *(starting to gather his things)* Okay, I've got to wrap up here and move on to my next meeting. This has been enlightening and exhilarating. Don't tell me--you planned to enlighten and exhilarate me didn't you?!

COACH: *(enjoying the humor)* No, but if that's what you got I'll take full credit for it!

BOB: I mean, where else would you learn this stuff? Acting class? Improv theatre? From my boss?

COACH: I don't know. We tend to pick this up naturally along the way. And some people just do it intuitively as a part of their talent. I just think there's a way to do it with more of a method--with more playfulness and purpose--that accelerates awareness and development.

NEXT STEPS TO ENACT

BOB: *(getting his pen for some concluding notes)* What do you see as my next step?

COACH: Sounds like you've got a good handle on playing actions, and structuring your action to get what you want, and help your audience get what they want, a win-win for both.

BOB: I'd agree.

COACH: I would suggest that you keep on simply noticing how this plays out for you, to start. Then, purposefully structure a real action plan or as in the actor's world, a structure of action for your scene--for one of the interactions you have coming up, and before we next meet.

BOB: Sounds good. I'd also like to try that Always, Sometimes, and Never chart for myself.

USING THE 4-A WAY OF COMMUNICATING

COACH: Great! Be aware, too, that action is one
component of what we've covered today. You might
want to think about the "4-A Way of Communicating",
something I put together to help people plan their
interactions:

AUDIENCE	ATMOSPHERE
What do I want from my audience? They from me?	What is the overall energy surrounding this interaction?

ACTOR	ACTION
Does my energy in body, voice, and intention support the action?	What am I doing to my audience to help us get what we want?

BOB: Great, Action is one--what are the other three?

COACH: Audience is first. Ask, "What does my
audience want from me, and what do I want from
them?" Then, consider the Atmosphere...

BOB: *(writing)* ...the second "A"...

COACH: ...of the situation, yes. Here it's, "What's the overall energy surrounding this interaction?" You've told me a lot about your Atmosphere today.

BOB: Probably a case of too much information!

COACH: No, that's fine! It helps you decide what actions to play. That's the third "A"--Action. The question here is about what you're doing to your audience to help them get what they want.

BOB: And the fourth?

COACH: Actor.

BOB: Uh-oh, that's about me. I'm an actor, improv actor, actor/leader....

COACH: *(enjoying this)* Not to worry, and you've already started down this path. There are many things to ask yourself here, but largely it's, "In body and voice am I supporting or taking away from the intended action?" And if you think about the actor in a theatre, it's everything from voice to costume to movement, to tone--the dynamic energy you portray to your audience.

BOB: *(gathering things)* I may need some help with that one.

COACH: I can help you with that.

BOB: You've been very helpful already and I appreciate your time today. I don't know where I'd get this anywhere else. Where else can I get feedback on these things that seem so fundamental! *(coming around the desk with notebook, pen, folder, and phone in hands)* I'm just looking forward to starting this action thing.

START NOW

COACH: Start now.

BOB: *(stopping)* Right now?

COACH: Start to notice the action going on in your next meeting, even as you walk down the hall.

BOB: I suppose I could.

COACH: *(getting the door for Bob)* Watch for action. Listen for action. Play your actions. From the start, when you greet the first person you see. What action will you play, at that moment?

BOB: *(pausing for a moment)* To…

COACH: *(extends hand to shake)* Until next time?

BOB: Yes. Thank you!

(Bob shuffles things around to free up his hand, the Coach and Bob shake hands as Bob hurries, actively, off)

END of PLAY

Action List

Following is a list of actions that can be played when engaging with an audience. By no means a comprehensive list, the actions listed are those that may be always, sometimes, or never played on your business stage. Remember that your role can be defined by actions selected so by reviewing the actions you may get an idea of a role you'd like to play now or in the future!

Accept	Arrest	Blindside
Accost	Assault	Boil
Acquaint	Assist	Bolster
Adjust	Attack	Bomb
Admire	Attract	Boost
Admit	Audit	Bore
Adopt	Avoid	Bother
Advise	Back	Bounce
Advocate	Badger	Box
Affront	Baffle	Brainwash
Aid	Bake	Break
Alert	Ban	Bribe
Allow	Banish	Bruise
Amuse	Bash	Brush
Analyze	Bat	Bug
Annoy	Bathe	Build
Appease	Battle	Bump
Applaud	Beg	Buoy
Appoint	Belittle	Burn
Appreciate	Betray	Bury
Approve	Blame	Calm
Arm	Blemish	Carry
Arouse	Bless	Carve

Cast	Cripple	Dress
Catch	Cross	Drive
Center	Crucify	Drop
Chaff	Crush	Drown
Challenge	Cure	Dry
Change	Damn	Dunk
Channel	Damage	Dust
Charge	Dare	Ease
Chase	Dazzle	Echo
Cheat	Deaden	Educate
Check	Debilitate	Electrify
Chew	Deceive	Eliminate
Choke	Decorate	Embarrass
Chop	Defy	Employ
Claim	Delay	Empower
Clean	Delight	Empty
Clear	Deliver	Enable
Clip	Denounce	Encourage
Close	Depress	Energize
Clutch	Desert	Engage
Coach	Destroy	Enjoy
Coddle	Detect	Enlighten
Color	Develop	Enlist
Command	Disarm	Enliven
Commission	Discipline	Enroll
Concern	Discourage	Entertain
Condition	Discover	Entitle
Confuse	Dismiss	Envy
Connect	Dislike	Examine
Consider	Dismember	Excite
Contain	Dismiss	Exclude
Control	Disregard	Excuse
Copy	Diss	Exhilarate
Correct	Dissuade	Exile
Cover	Doubt	Exonerate
Crack	Drag	Expel
Craze	Drain	Face

Fail	Harm	Involve
Fancy	Hassle	Irritate
Fasten	Hate	Isolate
Fear	Haunt	Jab
Fence	Heal	Jail
Fetch	Heat	Jam
Fill	Heed	Jerk
Fine	Help	Jog
Fire	Hinder	Join
Fix	Hit	Josh
Flood	Hold	Jostle
Focus	Hook	Judge
Follow	Humor	Juggle
Fool	Hunt	Jump
Force	Hurry	Kick
Form	Hypnotize	Kid
Fortify	Ignore	Kill
Fragment	Impede	Kiss
Frame	Impel	Knit
Frighten	Impress	Knock
Fry	Improve	Knot
Gag	Incite	Label
Glue	Include	Launch
Goad	Inflame	Lead
Grab	Influence	Let
Grate	Inform	Level
Grease	Inject	Lick
Greet	Injure	Lighten
Grip	Inspire	Like
Guarantee	Instruct	Limit
Guard	Insult	Lure
Guide	Interest	Madden
Hammer	Interrupt	Manage
Hamper	Intimidate	Manipulate
Handle	Introduce	Mark
Hang	Invigorate	Match
Harass	Invite	Measure

Melt	Paint	Provoke
Mesmerize	Pamper	Pull
Milk	Park	Pump
Mind	Pass	Punch
Miss	Paste	Puncture
Mobilize	Pat	Punish
Mold	Paw	Query
Monitor	Peck	Question
Motivate	Peel	Quiz
Move	Permit	Race
Mug	Pester	Raise
Murder	Pick	Ram
Nag	Pinch	Razz
Nail	Place	Reach
Name	Plant	Receive
Needle	Play	Recognize
Neglect	Please	Refuse
Note	Plug	Regard
Notice	Poke	Reject
Notify	Polish	Relax
Nullify	Pop	Release
Number	Possess	Relish
Nuzzle	Preempt	Remember
Obey	Prefer	Remind
Objectify	Prejudge	Remove
Observe	Prepare	Renew
Obtain	Present	Repair
Offend	Preserve	Replace
Offer	Press	Represent
Open	Pressure	Reprove
Order	Prick	Require
Ostracize	Prime	Rescue
Oust	Program	Restore
Owe	Promise	Retain
Own	Prompt	Retire
Pacify	Prop	Return
Paddle	Protect	Revive

Rinse	Signal	Strengthen
Rob	Skip	Stretch
Rock	Slap	Strip
Roll	Slam	Stroke
Rub	Slay	Stuff
Ruin	Slow	Submerge
Rule	Smash	Suck
Rush	Smite	Summon
Sack	Smoke	Supply
Satisfy	Snatch	Support
Save	Sniff	Surprise
Saw	Snow	Surround
Scare	Soak	Suspect
Scatter	Soothe	Suspend
School	Spank	Sustain
Scold	Spare	Sway
Scorch	Spark	Switch
Scrape	Spell	Tame
Scratch	Spoil	Tap
Screw	Spoof	Task
Scrub	Spot	Taste
Seal	Spray	Tax
Search	Squash	Teach
Secure	Squish	Tease
Seduce	Squeeze	Tell
Seize	Squelch	Tempt
Separate	Stain	Terrify
Serve	Stamp	Test
Settle	Startle	Thank
Shade	Stay	Thaw
Shape	Steer	Tickle
Share	Step	Tie
Shave	Stimulate	Time
Shelter	Stir	Tip
Shift	Stitch	Tolerate
Shock	Stop	Torment
Sicken	Strap	Touch

Tow	Unfasten	Watch
Trace	Unite	Water
Trade	Unlock	Weaken
Train	Unnerve	Weigh
Transport	Unseat	Welcome
Trap	Uphold	Whack
Trick	Upset	Whip
Trip	Urge	Wipe
Trot	Use	Wrestle
Trouble	Vex	Yank
Trust	Vilify	
Try	Vindicate	
Tug	Vitalize	
Tumble	Volunteer	
Turn	Want	
Tutor	Warm	
Twist	Warn	
Type	Wash	
Undress	Waste	

###